THE HISTORY OF FARMING IN AMERICA

History of the United
States Grade 6 |

Children's American
History

BABY PROFESSOR
EDUCATION KIDS

First Edition, 2021

Published in the United States by Speedy Publishing LLC, 40 E Main Street, Newark, Delaware 19711 USA.

© 2021 Baby Professor Books, an imprint of Speedy Publishing LLC

Baby Professor Books are available at special discounts when purchased in bulk for industrial and sales-promotional use. For details contact our Special Sales Team at Speedy Publishing LLC, 40 E Main Street, Newark, Delaware 19711 USA. Telephone (888) 248-4521 Fax: (210) 519-4043.

10 9 8 7 6 * 5 4 3 2 1

Print Edition: 9781541954861
Digital Edition: 9781541957862
Hardcover Edition: 9781541984318

See the world in pictures. Build your knowledge in style.
www.speedypublishing.com

TABLE OF CONTENTS

THE GREAT PLAINS IS A VAST EXPANSE OF OPEN GRASSLAND.

When European settlers arrived in America, they found a land rich in resources. Pushing beyond the original 13 colonies and past the Appalachian Mountains, explorers and settlers saw a vast expanse of open grassland – the Great Plains – that was ideal for farming.

There was so much space, in fact, that the government could give away free land. The United States flourished as an agricultural society, but there were several challenges facing American farmers in the late 1800s. By banding together, farmers found ways to improve their situations. Let's take a look at the history of farming in America.

THE UNITED STATES FLOURISHED AS AN AGRICULTURAL SOCIETY.

The Great Plains offered the ideal place for farming. Most of the region was covered in tall prairie grasses. There were few trees. Cattle could graze all summer.

IN THE GREAT PLAINS, CATTLE COULD GRAZE ALL SUMMER.

THERE WAS ENOUGH HAY TO FEED CATTLE IN THE WINTER.

Farmers cut and dried the prairie grasses into hay to feed their cattle in the wintertime.

HARVESTING WHEAT ON A BONANZA FARM IN DAKOTA TERRITORY.

The soil was rich and fertile. Farmers could grow corn, wheat, and other cash crops, as well as all the vegetables needed to feed their families.

HOMESTEADERS DROPPING SEEDS TO
SOW CORN ON THE GREAT PLAINS.

THERE WAS AN ABUNDANCE OF WILD GAME FOR HUNTING.

In addition, there were plenty of wild game for hunting. Deer, pheasants, turkey, rabbits, ducks, and antelope could be hunted for meat. Resources were abundant.

SETTLING THE GREAT PLAINS

In the mid-1800s, the United States government wanted to settle the Great Plains. People from the eastern cities were already moving to California and other parts of the west coast. Now it was time to settle the frontier region in the center of the country.

THE GREAT PLAINS OF THE UNITED STATES

The prevailing attitude of the time was Manifest Destiny. This was the belief that the United States was destined to settle all of North America. People thought that God wanted white European pioneers to settle the Great Plains, therefore they were justified in taking the land from the Native Americas who made their homes there.

A VISUAL REPRESENTATION OF THE CONCEPT OF MANIFEST DESTIN FEATURING AN ALLEGORICAL WHITE FEMALE.

To encourage people to move to the Great Plains with their families and start farms, the United States passed the Homestead Act of 1862.

THE HOMESTEAD ACT OF 1862 ENCOURAGED FAMILIES TO SETTLE THE WEST BY GIVING THEM LAND ALMOST FREE.

(1.)

HOMESTEAD.

APPLICATION } No.—— LAND OFFICE at——,——, 18

I,———, of———, do hereby apply to enter, under the provisions of the act of Congress approved May 20, 1862, entitled "An act to secure Homesteads to actual settlers on the public domain," the —— of Section ——, in Township —— of Range ——, containing —— acres

LAND OFFICE at——,——, 18 .

I ————, Register of the Land Office, do hereby certify that the above application is for Surveyed Lands of the class which the applicant is legally entitled to enter under the Homestead act of May 20, 1862, and that there is no prior, valid, adverse right to the same.

————
Register.

(2.)

HOMESTEAD.

(*Affidavit.*) LAND OFFICE at ——,

(*Date.*) ——

I,———— of ———— having filed my *Application No.*——, for an entry under the provisions of the act of Congress, approved May 20, 1862, entitled "An act to secure Homesteads to actual settlers on the public domain," do

solemnly swear, that [*Here state whether the applicant is the head of a family, or over twenty-one years of age; whether a citizen of the United States, or has filed his declaration of intention of becoming such; or, if under twenty-one years of age, that he has served not less than fourteen days in the army or navy of the United States during actual war; that said Application No.—— is made for his or her exclusive benefit; and that said entry is made for the purpose of actual settlement and cultivation, and not, directly or indirectly, for the use or benefit of any other person or persons whomsoever.*]

Sworn to and subscribed, this —— day of ——, before ——

————

[*Register or Receiver*] *of the Land Office.*

(3.)

MILITARY OR NAVAL HOMESTEAD.

APPLICATION } No.—— LAND OFFICE at ——,——, 186

I,———, of ————, being in the —— service of the United States, do hereby apply to enter, under the provisions of the act approved March 21, 1864, amendatory of the Homestead act of May 20, 1862, and for other purposes, a certain tract of land, which —— is hereby authorized to designate, at the foot of this application, as my Homestead, and which I agree to hold as my own selection.

ATTEST: ————, Commanding officer at ——,

APPLICATION FOR A HOMESTEAD PUBLISHED IN A CIRCULAR OF THE GENERAL LAND OFFICE.

Under this act, a U.S. citizen could claim 160 acres of land in the Great Plains. They had to pay a $10 filing fee at a land surveyor's office to make sure no one else had already claimed that land.

Once the homestead claim was filed in their name, the homesteader had to live on the land for five years. At the end of the five years, ownership of the land transferred from the U.S. government to the homesteader who now had 160 acres of free land. It may have been free land, but it wasn't easy to get.

PIONEER HOMESTEAD IN THE FAR WEST.

CHALLENGES TO HOMESTEADERS

IT TOOK TOUGH, DETERMINED, AND RESOURCEFUL PEOPLE
TO MAKE A LIVING ON HOMESTEAD CLAIMS.

Living on a homestead claim for five years was very difficult. Many settlers gave up, relinquished their claims, and moved back east. It took tough, determined, and resourceful people to make a living on homestead claims, especially during the first few years.

The roots of prairie grasses go deep into the ground. It was back-breaking work to plow the land to plant crops.

IT WAS BACK-BREAKING WORK TO PLOW THE LAND TO PLANT CROPS.

Often, the homestead claims were far away from the nearest towns. Loneliness took a toll on people. Even if a homesteader had his family with him, it was still an isolating experience. And, although the prairie offered a lot of resources, the lack of trees posed unique challenges, particularly when it came to housing.

EVEN IF A HOMESTEADER HAD HIS FAMILY WITH HIM, IT WAS STILL AN ISOLATING EXPERIENCE.

With few trees on the prairie, settlers had to either haul in lumber to build their homes – which was very expensive to do – or use the resources available to them. One option was to build a sod home. Squares of dirt, with the grass and roots intact, were cut and stacked to form the walls and roofs of sod homes.

A PIONEER FAMILY ALONGSIDE THEIR SOD HOUSE IN NEBRASKA.

A SOD HOUSE ON THE KANSAS GREAT PLAINS.

PRAIRIE HOMESTEAD FAMILY PREPARING FOR WINTER AT THEIR SOD HOME.

Sod houses, or soddies as they were called, were tiny, dark, and damp. When it rained, the house was leaking and muddy. The thick walls, however, kept out the wind and the snow.

BANKING A PRAIRIE FARM WITH SOD FOR THE WINTER. DAKOTA TERRITORY.

Other homesteaders built dugout homes. These were basically man made caves dug into hillsides. Like soddies, dugouts were crammed and dirty. Sod houses and dugouts were meant to be temporary houses until the homesteader was able to grow a good crop and sell it for profit.

A DUGOUT HOME COVERED WITH SOD FOR A PRAIRIE HOMESTEADER.

The promise of free land lured many people, especially poorer families, to the Great Plains. The introduction of the railroad brought even more settlers. The railroad, which linked the east coast and the west coast, ran through the Great Plains.

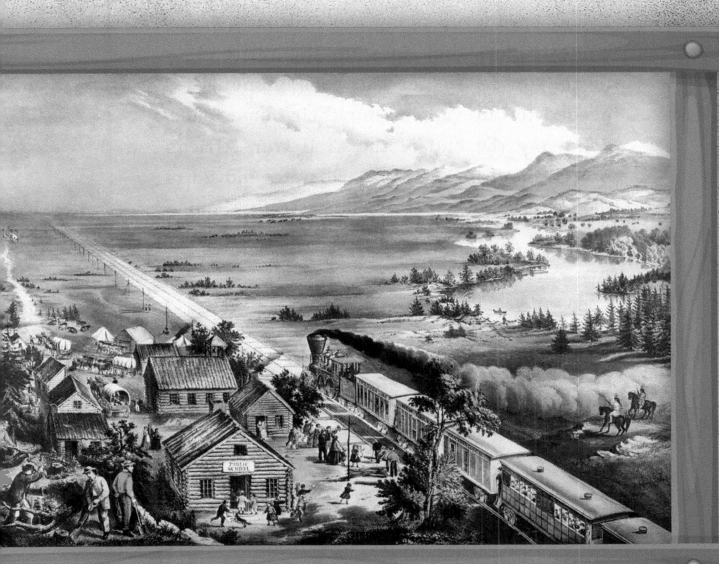

TRANSCONTINENTAL RAILROAD ACROSS THE GREAT PLAINS.

Towns sprang up along the railroads. Many homesteaders took jobs on the railroad or in the towns to get the cash money they needed to buy supplies for their homesteads. Following the end of the Civil War, African Americans from the southern states moved to the Great Plains to become homesteaders, too.

MANY HOMESTEADERS TOOK JOBS ON THE RAILROAD OR IN THE TOWNS TO GET THE CASH MONEY THEY NEEDED.

RAILROAD STOP NEAR A NEW TOWN ON THE GREAT PLAINS

AN UNDERGROUND VILLAGE OF DUGOUTS DOING BUSINESS
ALONG THE TRANSCONTINENTAL RAILROAD.

BY THE END OF THE 1800S, MORE THAN HALF A MILLION
SETTLERS MOVED TO HOMESTEAD FARMS.

For many people, the Homestead Act was the only way they could ever afford to own their own farmland. By the end of the 1800s, more than half a million settlers moved to homestead farms.

Life on the homestead meant constant work from sun up to sun down. For men and boys, their days were spent outdoors. They broke sod, plowed, tended the crops, and harvested the crops.

FARM BOY LEADING A TEAM OF HORSES WHILE HIS FATHER STEERS THE PLOW.

SETTLERS BUILDING A FENCE AROUND A
HOMESTEAD ON THE FRONTIER.

To get fresh water, they had to dig a well. They put up fences to keep the cattle pastured. When they needed fresh meat, the men or boys hunted and fished.

The women and girls were equally busy. They prepared meals. Much of the garden produce was preserved for the winter months. The women and girls made cheese, churned butter, collected eggs, washed clothes, baked bread, and cleaned the home. The quilts on the beds and the clothes that the family wore all had to be sewn by the women of the home.

THE WOMEN AND GIRLS TOOK CARE OF THE FAMILY BY MAKING MEALS, SEWING CLOTHES AND DOING HOUSE CHORES.

THE HOMESTEADERS WHO STUCK IT OUT ON THEIR HOMESTEAD
CLAIMS WERE REWARDED BY LAND OWNERSHIP.

The homesteaders who stuck it out on their homestead claims were rewarded by land ownership. For people who would not have had the opportunity to own farms back east, having a homestead was a source of pride. The sprawling cities of the east were crowded, noisy, and dirty.

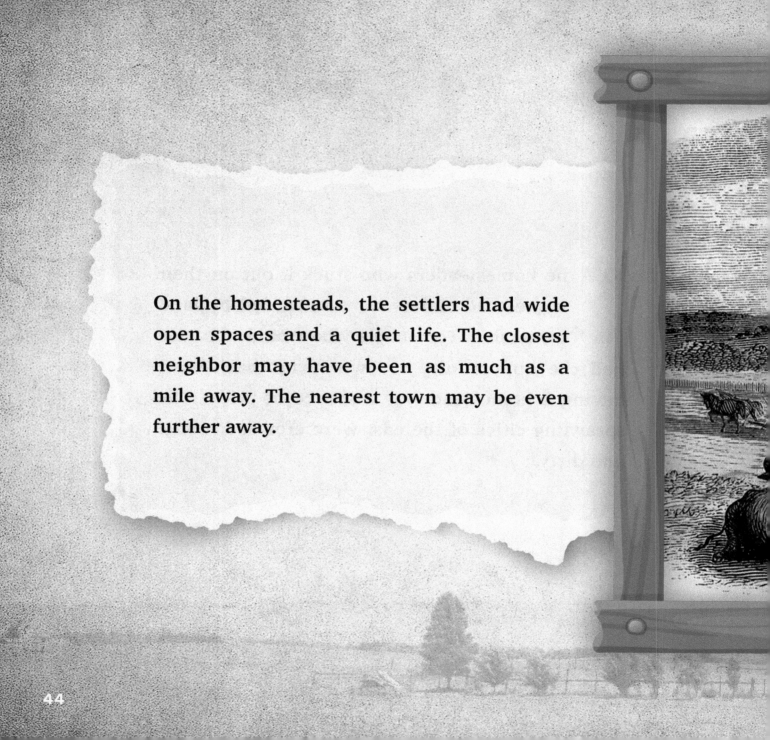

On the homesteads, the settlers had wide open spaces and a quiet life. The closest neighbor may have been as much as a mile away. The nearest town may be even further away.

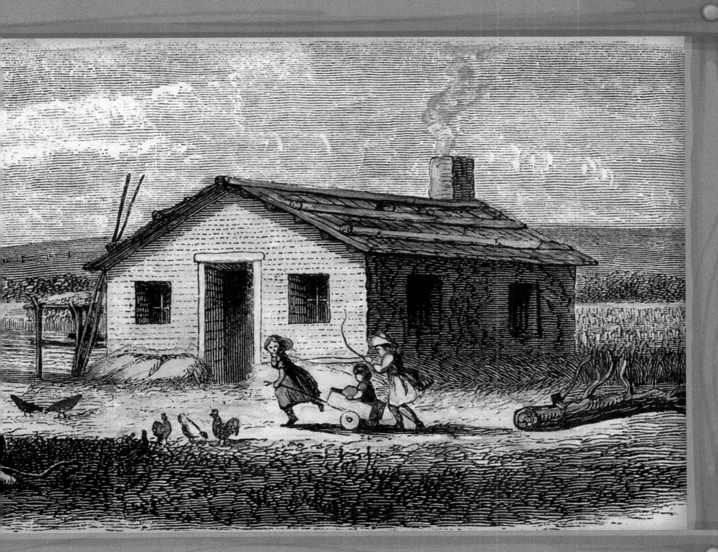

ON THE HOMESTEADS, THE SETTLERS HAD WIDE OPEN SPACES AND A QUIET LIFE.

PRAIRIE SETTLERS OFTEN CAME TOGETHER TO HELP EACH OTHER OUT.

Despite the distances, the farmers often relied on each other. When large projects arose, like harvesting the crops, the farmers came together to help each other out.

n the last half of the 1800s, several inventions were introduced that helped American farmers. One was a steel plow that was invented by James Oliver in 1877.

JAMES OLIVER

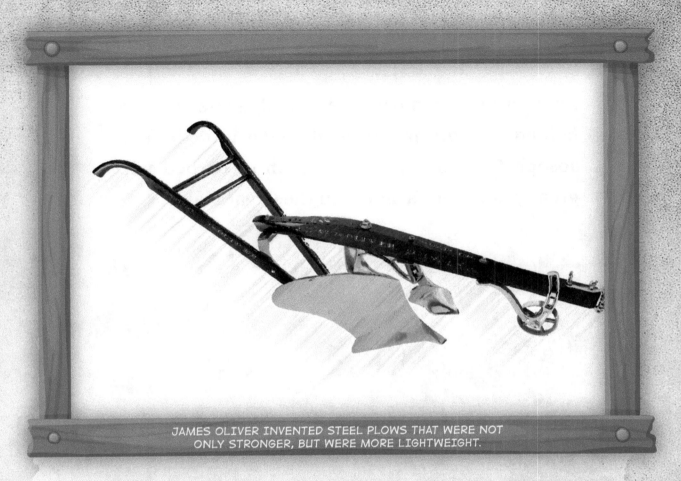

JAMES OLIVER INVENTED STEEL PLOWS THAT WERE NOT
ONLY STRONGER, BUT WERE MORE LIGHTWEIGHT.

The tangle of roots of the prairie grasses were difficult for the traditional iron plows to dig through. The sod was so thick that iron plows broke apart. The steel plows were not only stronger, they were more lightweight. They were easier for the horses to pull.

Another invention was a seed drill, a machine that helped farmers insert seeds deep into the soil. Joseph Glidden's 1874 invention of barbed wire greatly changed farm life in the Great Plains.

A SEED DRILL IS A MACHINE THAT HELPED FARMERS INSERT SEEDS DEEP INTO THE SOIL.

JOSEPH GLIDDEN

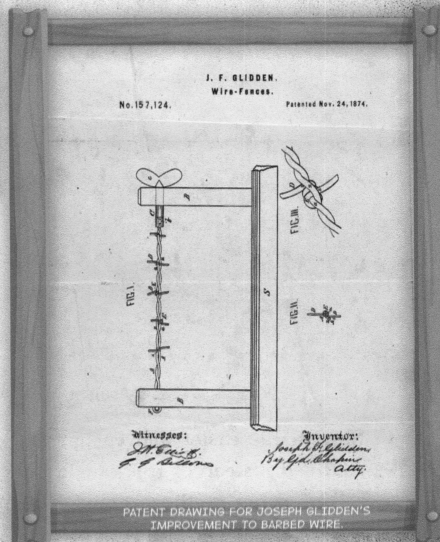

J. F. GLIDDEN.
Wire-Fences.

No. 157,124.

Patented Nov. 24, 1874.

FIG. 1.

FIG. III.

FIG. II.

Witnesses:

Inventor:
Joseph F. Glidden
By G. L. Chapin
Atty.

PATENT DRAWING FOR JOSEPH GLIDDEN'S
IMPROVEMENT TO BARBED WIRE.

A BARBED WIRE FENCE SEEN AT THE BOUNDARY OF A FARM.

Now it was easier and cheaper to keep cattle confined instead of free-ranging them. All this solved many of the problems facing farmers in America.

Farming in the Great Plains pitted the farmers against the forces of nature. In the winter, blizzards dumped feet of snow on the homesteads.

A SOD HOUSE AND OUTBUILDINGS DURING A SNOWSTORM IN THE WESTERN PRAIRIE.

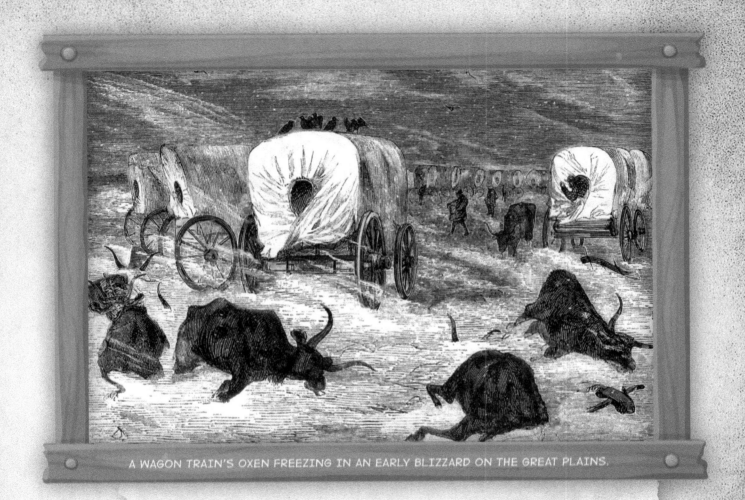

A WAGON TRAIN'S OXEN FREEZING IN AN EARLY BLIZZARD ON THE GREAT PLAINS.

Cattle was buried in snow drifts. Families were stranded in their homes for months.

THE GREAT PLAINS WERE PRONE TO TERRIBLE AND DESTRUCTIVE STORMS, INCLUDING TORNADOES.

In the summer months, the Great Plains were prone to terrible and destructive storms, including hail storms and tornadoes. Rivers and creeks occasionally flooded the farmlands.

There were other, unexpected forces, too. In the 1870s, swarms of grasshoppers destroyed farm crops. There were so many grasshoppers that they destroyed all the plants in an area. They even ate the fence posts, wooden wagon wheels, and laundry on the clothesline.

IN THE 1870S, SWARMS OF GRASSHOPPERS DESTROYED FARM CROPS.

FARMERS FIGHTING A GRASSHOPPER PLAGUE IN KANSAS IN 1875.

As more and more homesteaders settled in different areas, towns were founded. Homesteaders gathered together to attend church and social functions. As people got to know their neighbors, they decided to band together to help each other.

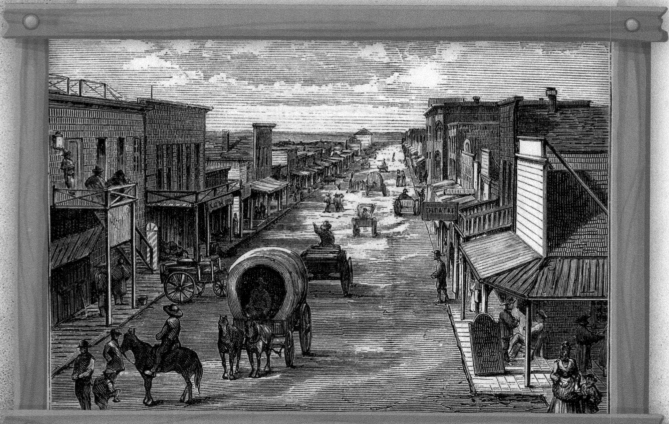

AS MORE AND MORE HOMESTEADERS SETTLED IN DIFFERENT AREAS, TOWNS WERE FOUNDED.

HOMESTEADERS GATHERED TOGETHER TO ATTEND CHURCH AND SOCIAL FUNCTIONS.

Events like threshing parties and barn raisings were ways for farmers to work together to tackle large jobs while using them as excuses for entertainment. When farmers banded together, they could solve many of their problems. It gave them more manpower. It also alleviated the loneliness and isolation that homesteaders experienced.

WHEN FARMERS BANDED TOGETHER, THEY COULD SOLVE MANY OF THEIR PROBLEMS.

hen the railroads were built across the Great Plains, it gave farmers a way to ship their crops to market faster and more efficiently. Trains helped to link the small towns of the frontier together.

TRAINS HELPED TO LINK THE SMALL TOWNS OF THE FRONTIER TOGETHER.

WORKERS WIRING TELEGRAPH POLES ALONG THE TRANSCONTINENTAL RAILROAD ON THE GREAT PLAINS.

Later, telegraph lines were strung from pole to pole across the country. The telegraph helped families stay connected with family members in other towns. It also helped farmers to arrange the sale of their goods to buyers in the cities.

A PONY EXPRESS RIDER PASSING WORKERS RAISING TELEGRAPH POLES ON THE GREAT PLAINS.

THE TELEGRAPH HELPED FAMILIES STAY CONNECTED WITH FAMILY MEMBERS IN OTHER TOWNS.

THE GREAT PLAINS HAS BEEN NICKNAMED "AMERICA'S BREAD BASKET" BECAUSE OF ALL THE WHEAT THAT IS GROWN THERE.

Trains and telegraphs also helped to make the lives of American farmers in the 1800s easier. America is still a world leader in agriculture even though most Americans no longer live on farms. The Great Plains has been nicknamed "America's Bread Basket" because of all the wheat that is grown there.

The United States, particularly the Great Plains, is rich in fertile farmland. The Homestead Act provided 160 acres of free land to any citizen so long as they could live on the land for five years. About half a million people moved to the prairie states from the crowded east coast cities to become farmers in the Great Plains. Life as a homesteader was difficult and full of challenges, but the farmers made their work easier by using new inventions, like barbed wire and steel plows. They also worked together to tackle large jobs.

Visit

www.speedypublishing.com

To view and download free content on your favorite subject and browse our catalog of new and exciting books for readers of all ages.

Printed in the USA
CPSIA information can be obtained
at www.ICGtesting.com
LVHW050528051023
760124LV00007B/231